20 Years

by

Sonja Lynn Williams

The contents of this work including, but not limited to, the accuracy of events, people, and places depicted; opinions expressed; permission to use previously published materials included; and any advice given or actions advocated are solely the responsibility of the author, who assumes all liability for said work and indemnifies the publisher against any claims stemming from publication of the work.

All Rights Reserved
Copyright © 2014 by Sonja Lynn Williams

No part of this book may be reproduced or transmitted, downloaded, distributed, reverse engineered, or stored in or introduced into any information storage and retrieval system, in any form or by any means, including photocopying and recording, whether electronic or mechanical, now known or hereinafter invented without permission in writing from the publisher.

Dorrance Publishing Co
701 Smithfield Street
Pittsburgh, PA 15222
Visit our website at www.dorrancebookstore.com

ISBN: 978-1-4349-3749-0
eISBN: 978-1-4349-3850-0

Dedication

I, Sonja Lynn Williams, would like to dedicate my second poetry book to my brother Gary Lee Williams. I've not seen my brother in 20 years of my life. Gary was born March 19, 1973 and I was born February 23, 1970. Both went separate ways, but I didn't know it would take half of my life to see my brother again. I want to go on with my life since God has lifted this burden off me...

Introduction

I would like to introduce my book to the publishing company. I give my talent, effort, and thanks to the company. As for the public, I thank you for your time and undivided attention to open the pages and read about my family and I. You may or may not become emotional from the beginning to the end. I hope you can feel my pain and over all sincerity in this book.

Let Me Tell You How I Feel

Let me tell you how I feel
It's hard for a nigga to be black
And real
I'm going to tell you about
How my brother and I lived about
The feelings I'm giving
About the roughness we're living
The reason why
I'm tell you not to cry
The pain, hurt, and scuffle
To deal my cards you must shuffle
Before I start my book off
You must know the publishing company
Is my boss
As I stated introducing all of you
To my feelings and your napkins
To put you down with what's happening.

Big Apple

Mother, brother, and her boyfriend moved to New York
Had no fishing rods, sinkers, and corks
Only a handful of clothes and furniture items
Inside riding in Buicks and Nissans
Where mosquitoes couldn't bite them
During the time I didn't go
I'm telling you so
They moved to Flatbush by Sunset Park
I went up there one night it was dark
My mom riding around looking for me
I was at little park making friends that she couldn't see
Later I went in but first I had to get my drink on
There was a child of mine I had born
Mother questioned me where I had been
Cause she said she drove around the block again
I told mom she didn't look in the right spots
I was visiting the family at the Big Apple red hot
In New York City, the Big Apple red hot.

Footnote: This was in Brooklyn, New York.

My Baby Boy

I had a son May 15, 1991
A newborn not old enough to eat a bun
First sound he made was a cry
I had to rock him side to side and pacify
He had fat puffy cheeks
And white looking feet
He loved smiling with his left leg cocked up
Right leg down not strong enough to hold a cup
My little one left me with a bikini cut
Every day the family and I changed his butt
His name is Marcus then full of joy
He is still my baby boy

Footnote: My son was born at M.C.V. in Richmond, Virginia and went to Brooklyn, New York with my mother.

The Fall in Po River

My family and I went fishing
We refused to listen
My brother and I played around the steep banks
My brother slipped and fell I didn't know what to think
I screamed daddy he is falling
Dad threw his fishing rod on the rocks after I was calling
He scolded, 'I told you to stop playing around the water'
That was his final order
He pulled Gary out he was full of fear
Heart beating fast water dripping from his ears
Eyes big and red
Like he's been swimming instead
Later on he got cold and started to shiver
All because of the fall in Po River.

Footnote: The river located at Thornburg, Virginia.

Gary

Gary was born March, 19 1973
Three years after me
Same zodiac sign called Pisces the fish
What I'm putting on paper no voices from a satellite dish
My brother has a heart of gold
Today he is 39-years-old
Grew up with my brother watching only his younger days
As I got older I couldn't see his new ways
I couldn't understand
Now I am a woman he is a man
Feelings and thoughts he left behind at a standstill
Family and friends from home looking out of the windowsill
They question the family members where is Gary?
I miss how he used to play
From back in the day.

The Park

Brother and I lived in a black and white house
Living nice like whites no cats or mouse
In the backyard two or three sheds
Where our pet dogs lived not dead
One with tools two full of clothes
In the back where we poked holes
In the ground and out
With a stick or piece of tree limb running about
I got on my knees with a piece of broken square
Wood not steel
Making dirt roads and dirt driveways for my brother that's for real
We were dirty and I remember the fun pushing matchbox cars
On our knees with lots of scars
My cousin would make grass houses to play with frogs
They were grown from birth of pollywogs
This happened before dark
During the summertime in our park.

Hamsford Hangout

My family and cousins used to go down Hamsford
To go swimming and eat crabs when we were bored
People drive their cars through the creek
Where the other side of the road meets
When I was six or seven
My uncle and dad used to drive us down
Hamsford before or after eleven
They would drink booze or be sipping
When we arrive to the scene whites skinny-dipping
My uncle pulls out his pistol or gun
Scare the hell out of everyone
Quickly they jump out leaving britches behind
We were just young kids who wanted some playtime
With a little splashing of water and shout
At the Hamsford Hangout

Bicycle Raceway

My Brother and I along with our cousins used grandfather's house
Raced our bicycles around it in circles until he cursed us out
Sometimes he would get his shotgun or wake up out of his sleep
We would run away, laugh at him, and creep
One day my grandfather shot through the front door we call him Johnny
Our dad scold us, but the shot hole wasn't tiny
We did the raceway for the longest later on we stopped
Cause we loved our Grandpop

Footnote: We lived in Spotsylvania, Virginia
On Route 645, Sunset Road

The Firecracker

I remember I was age ten
It was the fourth of July then
We were outside at night lighting cherry bombs
My baby brother threw one
It went between my legs
All I could do was holler not beg
So I started crying
My brother got a beaten for lying
That night my dad was a wacker
About the firecracker

The Haircut I Gave Myself

At eight-years-old I had long hair
Blew like a white girl in the air
One day my mom wouldn't comb it when I was ready
I didn't see my daddy
I went in the room found the scissors
I started cutting hair no whiskers
Mom yelled, 'No you didn't cut your hair'
She got the belt beat me all over and under chairs
All around the bed and left welts
Because I gave a haircut to myself.

The Egg

I was two when I used to watch my mother cook
I was a baby I learned from looks
I used a chair to put up to the stove
At two-years-old
I opened the door of the refrigerator to use butter I didn't use lard
Too young to think hard
Mom and Dad were in their room
I stood in the chair next to the stove was the broom
I cracked an egg and poured it out of the shell in the frying pan
She ran to get the camera took a picture using both hands
All I could see Mom and Dad smiles
To see the picture again would be worthwhile
I didn't get down with my legs
I was held from cooking the egg.

Footnote: At home in Spotsylvania, Virginia.

Tim's Truck

I believe I was fifteen or sixteen years of age
My brother was at a mischievous stage
Gary would hang out by Indian Acres
Many people we knew labeled Gary as a troublemaker
I didn't remember my brother's partner
He went over old man Tim Coleman's house a well-known Gardner
Gary had a misunderstanding with him
The last I heard he set a fire a truck that belonged to Tim
They called my mom
My mother got her switch called hot Tom
Gave my brother a whipping no matter what
For blowing up the truck

Left Alone

Mom and Dad went their separate ways
I knew this would be the last of family days
Broken up from fights, anger, and misery
The feelings I carried was bitterly
I was sixteen going on seventeen
The worst I had ever seen
My brother went to Richmond I was in Spotsylvania
That's where we were from
A small county where they filmed *Roots*
Back in the day with homemade basketball hoops
Made of bicycle rim, shoestrings, or rope
I was debating on where to move I hope
I was still under my mother's care
The after effects of our broken family was still in me what a scare
The feelings will always live in me I mean never gone
Of how I was left alone

Barrett Home for Boys

A long driveway surrounded by lots of trees
A place called Barrett where my brother was taken from me
Remember I told you my brother set a truck on fire
There we drove on a dirt road between honeysuckle
bushes with fences of barbwire
A big yard full of boys
Running around no small toys
Playing among themselves outside a big white brick house
Hard tile floors with aluminum chairs nothing soft as a couch
We rode in my dads Chevrolet nova
Pretty green grass where I couldn't see four leaf clovers
Time is all he could inherit
In Hanover, Virginia a home for boys called Barrett.

A Wish for Our Mother's Love

Two of mother's children watering at the mouth
Raised partially down south
We grew up living off beatings
From my mother when she thought my father was cheating
I could no longer stand by the family's side
For no reason we would cry
Sometimes tears of pain
We thought our parents were insane
Our mother turns elsewhere
Today we seem not to care
More than anything including stars above
My brother and I wish for our mothers love.

The Crawling of a Black Snake

I was young at the creek
Where we go hang out and meet
During the time I was four
Plenty of water to splash and much more
My mother walked to another part of the water she couldn't swim
I played with my brother in the cradle a snake crawled in beside him
I yelled. "Mom a snake is next to my brother"
She said, "Don't move no further"
She grabbed a stick
Long but not too thick
Quickly used the tip
To go midway under his body with a flip
My mom didn't want the snake to bite
Her baby that was insight
The snake got away wiggling downstream
From the yelling and screams
My little heart couldn't take
The crawling of a black snake.

The Second Term Felon

Living on Route three Salem Run Station
Working at Bekin's moving company with a girl of bad relations
Money was okay but then good
Moving furniture thick hardwood
I lived with a bondsman he looked out for me and my girl
And he was license to carry a double barrel
I waited for this chick out of prison
Fast and hardheaded from Orange Virginia but she still wouldn't listen
I had her before Dolly I am glad I left
I didn't like the way she made me felt
I thought I was sleeping with an enemy like the movie
She was a thief nothing fly or groovy
Later in the town of Orange I stabbed a girl that wasn't right
But the girl followed me all night
I went to jail
Couldn't get out on bail
My so-called girl was the snitch
I continued to be with this bitch
She testified against me in two cases
I was hurt didn't want to face it
In 2011 she sent me an apology
Stating she lied that was my life and freedom not biology
I am only telling
How I was back in the system as a second term felon.

My Isuzu

Summer of 1999
Worked for Bekin's always on time
Every day I drove from Fredericksburg to Woodbridge
Sometimes I would grab something cold out of the fridge
Whether its soda or beer
Talking trash on the way full of cheer
The car my girl and I drove was an Isuzu similar to a Stylus
One day I went to work thinking Jimmy would fire us
He assigned me to a job alone
It was 5000 pounds I waited for no one I was gone
I didn't know that I had that much power
I finish the job in seven hours
My supervisor was amazed
Nearly three weeks later I received a raise
The muscles I have I cant pretend
But I was strong like men
No slouch or wildcat
Respected and loved for that

Family Roll

Just like my hands my feelings are wash
Its sad the way the family roll against each other like trash
Straight talk now break the ice
To be honest it's nothing nice
Let me tell you so
About long ago
A handful would babysit us at my mothers
Before I go further
I would throw a fit
They would feed us pork n beans or a catsup sandwich
Worst I had ever seen
To be that mean
Some thought they were all of that
Today money wise I am trying to make my pockets fat
Writing books and news media
But I can't feed ya
I know how to get the dollar
Not jealous but wear the polo collar
I am not down for whatever
I can say never
New cars and clothes doesn't phase me
You niggas should praise me
No time for your pity
That's why I have made a family with my girl who is pretty
Your ways have played out and old
That's how you family roll.

Life Without My Brother

As time flies
Years went by
May be 5 or 6 I did prison time caught up in the
Mix Sometimes my brother visit same as show
He couldn't find me cause he didn't know
I had just started living my adulthood life
Still getting in trouble no husband or wife.
Knowing I wasn't a child walking a pup
I was just growing up.

Loving Lucille

Ear to ear all smiles
Sometimes she is known for putting food on her table
In piles
A country girl who knows how to put it down
Loves playing the blues with high-pitch music sounds
So much laughter and fun
Out of all she is my cousin the favorite one
There is no way you could hate
She is real not fake
Always good for conversing
Overall, she is a loving person.

Life at Huntington Circle

A village of Negroes off Post Office Road
Lived there before me riding with their families in car loads
Prices just as high in the city no cheaper
Nothing but all blacks no white people
I lived at Jesmond Court during the part of year 2007
A woman with four kids I thought life was like heaven
I worked at the Old Union 76 Truck Stop by Harry Nice Bridge
In Newburg, Maryland where most have taken their lives jumping off the ridge
I was a waitress and bartender all in one
But my love life was no fun
I helped my German girlfriend from paycheck to paycheck
My life was a total wreck
Couldn't go in her family's house she would sneak me in
Cause her family and I weren't friends
Her sister was nice and fine pretty looking but she wasn't mine
We split up I was relieved from a miracle
This was part of my life at Huntington Circle.

Charles County Days

I lived for one year in Waldorf Maryland
A short hair cut with no curls
We had a joint bank account and a four-bedroom duplex home
She had four kids me and wasn't alone
She loved the kids well
They gave me hell
My girl had a private nursing job
But she was tall and large
The times I didn't babysit they would go to their father's in Virginia and La Plata
Sometimes that was the only way I could date her
Together the four kids with two no-good dads
Felt that's all they had
Never paid child support
That's why I worked at the truck stop when leaving Jesmond Court
Later on we fell apart
Broke each other's hearts
I bought a laptop Dell
Hit her with it her face started to swell
Went to the floor off our feet
They called the police
I got locked up in Charles County Detention Center
During the summer time no longer winter
My father bonded me out
But later asked what was this all about
We talked Dad told me to change my ways
You are living in Charles County days.

Section 8 Girl

I filled out an application
One day at A.J.'s station
Three weeks went by I was hired as part time
I knew I had to walk a straight line
But I was a hard worker no type of pretender
I worked inside the ware house met a woman name Brenda
She seemed to be cool
But she was old school
One Saturday she came to J.B. apartments next to Pinefield
I was inside eating no food on the grill
A little girl knocked at the door
As I walked across the floor
I asked whose little girl are you?
She told me her name was Aaliyah you work with my mom that's true
Brenda came in
Told me she wanted to be my friend
I guess she liked my style
I'm young with an old soul not as wild
But I do have it in me like the rest of the world
Speaking on pieces of life about the section 8 girl.

The South East fight

Summer of 2007 I was in D.C.
Until I moved with Brenda in southeast
She lived off Gainesville
She would always look out the window arms folded on the windowsill
Her daughter was young
Always wanted to have fun
I went to northwest with a friend who wasn't gay
One day in June of 2008
I had to go back to southside for my clothes
We argued I called her hoes
I hit her first and slammed her against the fence
Outside I slipped she had me pinned
I got up she gave a push down concrete steps
Pain was all I felt
I had to go to Greater Southeast Hospital from a dislocated joint
She put me out I had no turning point
When we fought they stood around like a boxing ring
On Gainesville where I used to hang.

The Sidewalk Hustle

I came out of the blue to Georgetown
Hustling people for money looking around
I often sit on crates
Early mornings or late
A little help or I'm homeless
I was offered Styrofoam dinners some was boneless
Some hustlers I hung with gave me a signal or a wink
I went to Blues Alley for a drink
They smoke or wanted to get their gage up
Sipping liquor and beer in white cups
Arms covered not showing any muscles
I went back out for a sidewalk hustle.

Footnote: In Georgetown northwest of Washington, D.C.

Streets of D.C.

I am giving it to you raw about D.C.
Coming straight from the heart of me
Since I have been in D.C. I lace
I have also seen so-called friends with dicks in their face
Sucking lapping men on men
Asking me to watch for them
I thought a woman would be the one
Instead I see a man go down for some
For a hit or that's his thrill
Play games or say I will
Its unbelievable but it is true
For men to be engaged too
Men dress like fems
Just know not to mention it to him
Best way to go
Is know how to flow
Just be alert look around
Don't forget the crack baggies on the ground
See and don't see if not expect a slash or a hole
From the blade or bullet of gold
Baby sitters molesting or even teachers
Hold on I can't forget about the preachers
The biggest crime of D.C. seems to be congested
Children being sexually molested
Others may not want to hear it or feel
They may be doing it I'm being real
Lesbians gritting on another dom.
Cause she doesn't think she'll have her girl too long
Only if someone else comes her way
To give her the right kind of play
You can't walk down the street without getting hated
All styles of shirts tye-dye or faded
Youngsters riding underground subways from line to line
Robbing anybody taking stolen goods of yours not mines
Homeless people living in cardboard homes
Messy and smelly living alone
Day by day still the same

This sad situation nothing but guilt and shame
I see why drug dealers sell to get by
The economy is tight and dry
Government officials steal money counted in layers
Some going down what about the now to be mayor
A house full of blacks no kin
Miscalculating figures behind the president and congressman
Away from the sidewalks of D.C.
Under a roof to be
Inside a room a office paper work and pleas
A house above a foundation in the streets of D.C.

Off the Streets

Lined up with a homeless survey
One night one day
Asked several questions if I get a place
Where would they find me or trace
What would I do with myself
Eat right stay in good health
At first this wasn't the way
But I have to say
It was god who wanted me to slow down from being hurt
Or have my face covered with dirt
I was transferred from a street survey to out reach of golden triangle
I had to talk mix and mingle
I was told I had an apartment I didn't believe
The answers and remarks I didn't want to receive
I kept walking away but October 2008 I was blessed
Living at the berks one of the best
Housed with community connections
A time of my perfection
Good above my head beneath my feet
A roof has me off the streets.

The Last Unknown

As I have gotten older
The winters are no longer colder
My age has made a difference
Years have gone by I have not seen my brother since
He wasn't a man
Old enough to understand
Before he left on the go
I didn't even know
It was gonna be the last visit
Today I still miss it.

The Hate Crime

In September 2011 I walk with my cane
Down a sidewalk one lane
With an associate on his too
I should have known that he didn't have a bright I.Q.
A baldy got into my conversation
Right below the Glover Park gas station
Accused of beating a nigga down built like Chuck Norris
When a nigga was taking a karate course
But ashamed to show up in court
And lied on me after he fought
I was sent to harbor lights
This crime I couldn't fight
A police officer blue under his collar
Just an uncle tom for another dollar
D.C. officers are crooked racial and slick
I often read about they are being fired and locked up for tricks
I love when authority don't know me but truthfully hates
They are the ones whose lives are on the line working late
They should really be scared of youngsters and hoods
I wish that youngsters could keep the officers on my side off me for good
I am going on with my life and 40 hours
And keep my pen and paper in power
For real I am no slouch or couch potato
I love my haters
I thank God for this head on my shoulder
To write a second book get money and learn to fold 'em
Overall I didn't get a chance to milk the system or do time
From a so-called hate crime.

Shorty

Just below the blue Virginia skies
There was my brother and I
My mom left
Couldn't be with no one else
We were still minors
Almost grown kind of
Lived in Richmond on Roane Street off Chamberlayne Avenue
You ought to see the things they push me to
I started selling drugs
Keeping my money under rugs
Working at McDonald's and across the street at the Shell Station
As a service station attendant and cashier no experience for a brick mason
My brother and I lived with a mechanic name Shorty
A lot older than us I didn't know if he was forty
He gave the family love and money
Nice trying to be a second dad but my moms honey
The reason I called this Shorty he's been around for years
We are still bouncing back to him with cheers.

Lifeless

My brother was in a street fight
In Brooklyn one night
Alcohol played a major role
I think the move was very cold
Caught off guard in a apartment building
My brother laid flat on his back looking at death towards the ceiling
No phone calls to make
Blood on the floor in layers like cake
48 hours around the clock
Bleeding from the brain veins to the heart
The paramedics asked what happened
He couldn't even hear sounds of tapping
Gary couldn't talk or respond
Doctors wondering why he laid under the staircase so long
Tubes running out of his head and nose
Cause the nigga threw some hard blows
He was paralyzed temporarily
Why would someone do this to Gary
Nurses and housekeepers cleaned up moving rugs
I felt for my brother who almost went to the morgue
Before I close I am hurt because I didn't know
Brother took it hard
All he could do was look up to thoughtless, but he had God.

My Fish Truck

After the serious injury that almost led to death
My brother had problems stuttering under his breath
Before and after he drove a fish truck
Still having bad luck
He tried to run his enemy over
Drinking heavy not sober
No longer using the fish truck for work
Cause of the way he was hurt
If I were there I would have tried to kill him out of spite
Cause the nigga almost took my brothers life
My brother drove through alleys for short cuts
To reach his goal doing crimes with the fish truck.

Life in New York

The city of New York is where my other sibling lived
But brother loved to give
A crazy woman in his life hard to dine
I never seen her, but he thought she was fine
He was stabbed in the thigh twice
Had thoughts of her being nice
Almost hit a main vessel
Didn't fight her or wrestle
He moved on to a white queen
Thought the world of her sweet like vanilla crème
He would often get drunk
At times ride bikes over humps
Fell asleep on a few got hit by cars
Some left him with life threatening scars
Scheduled for a hip replacement from accidents
Never cross his mind God was giving hints
Can't run, but can jog
Never mentioned if the medicine made him nod
Worked on a car for my mom's ex
Let me tell you what happened next
The car caught on fire
From the motor and wires
My brother was burnt 123-degree burns
What a valuable lesson to learn
Life been in danger from every move he made
From games people played
Shouldn't have tried to do every thing
Next time put your foot down to be the king
Later on my brother built a racecar by himself
Raced it up and down the streets with some one else
Engine roaring back then
My brother told me it was stolen
Cant hold the knife in the left hand tight sitting on a table along with the fork
You are in prison from the life you lived in New York.

Life Without You

From New York to Fredericksburg
My brother stopped through couldn't get the sound of a word
When asking about Sonja on every visit from every ride
Some of the family lied
Wouldn't come straight forward
In the future they must answer to the lord
Continue to live your brother hood
Looking up to your sister like a brother should
Don't keep worrying about the rest
Please know it's a good thing to worry less
No good has surfaced since you left years ago
Family and associates need to know
As long as you have been gone
It hurts being alone
But the longtime hit shocked their nerves
Even though they haven't seen you or heard
Many thought you were dead
They are only good for thinking bad
I am still down to earth and true
There is no life without you.

The Lead Pipe

A year or two later
My brother's emotions turned alligator
Hit a nigga in the face
In New York some place
Some where on the side of a street
Took a lead pipe knocked the nigga off his feet
Broke his nose fractured his eye socket
Used the stranger as his target
Also broke his jaw
Violated the New York law
First-degree assault not quite attempted murder
Stayed free until the judge reached a verdict
Free for a year in a half or two
Now serving time his white girl bought everything new
Sentence to three years and will be on three years parole
That's what I have been told
A big boy no more tears to wipe
Placed in the president's house from using a lead pipe.

My Brother's Pain

I am your sister I am not the same
I am concerned about your pain
Every day in life we view
There is no way I can be you
You said the family drove new cars back in the day
You know we didn't deserve to be treated that way
Don't even let them think we are jealous
On the side like one of the fellas
If you were left out
Don't you think I was the same no doubt?
Both now faraway they must take grey hound or train
A good feeling to be away from the insane
Give up not on life but release to Jesus
Its going to be with us
For the rest of our lives
Let go of the swords and knives
You have to live with yourself
Not inside of no one else
I hurt just as bad
Forgive the family Mom and Dad
Sometimes we don't know how to understand
Today we don't have to live on the same land
Just make peace
Before departing this earth at least
The old saying put up your guns
But you don't have to aim
I love you brother cause I feel your pain.

Getting It Together

The crime has gone up higher in rates
My brother and I been in system in different states
For a long time
We must keep trying
Stay out slammers and faces
And keep our lives in place
Be cool relaxed and mellow
By getting it together.

The Day of April 26 2012

The day of April 26 2012
My heart start to melt
This was the day I cried
I had a buddy of mine by my side
My brother wrote me a letter
I was relieved but I felt better
Because this was a search that cause me part of my life
Looking for him day and night
From this day tears drip
Every letter I have gotten but couldn't rip
All I could do was look on the floor
And cry some more
But I am so glad
From the April 26 letter I read.

A Message to Blacks and Whites

I am not all that well
But I am here to say I am not a prejudice gal
When people look at me
Some get bad vibes you cant see
Either they are just hating or feel threatening
Whites and blacks I am not sweating
I am looking at two sides of the world as one
I am speaking on your complexion
Don't get me wrong I must be right
It is better to deal with whites
They really don't turn or kill each other like we do
The reason I wrote this we should all on both sides pull each other through.

Rebecca

A lady's name she's been holding since birth
She's the best in the family as well as on Earth
I want to thank her for searching the web
Cause I wanted to find my brother real bad
Many say reap what you sow
With Rebecca you cant she is good to know
Always wear a smile
But loves to care for a child
I am glad she's family and I met her
A wonderful woman, Rebecca.

Reunited

Gary lived the way he felt was needed
Upstate New York down to Washington D.C. yes indeed
Stabbings up north to a push down the steps
A sister and brother who had no help
Long distance the two didn't have a contact
For years didn't know about each other true facts
Couldn't reach out for favors
Today, we are both disabled
A letter through the mail broke the news I was excited
Sonja and Gary have finally reunited.

Thanks for Finding Me

Across the waters
Through different borders
There was a young man fighting other inmates at Governor Facility
Couldn't beat them all didn't have the capability
He was transferred in mid-April
But still on papers
Received letters from a sister and cousin
Arrived in Malone, New York cause he fought dozens
A blessing but a life savior as you can see
My brother said thanks for finding me.

Bare Hill Correctional Facility

Walls with some graffiti
Steel bars too tough you can't beat 'em
Toilet seat is ice cold like ice water in a glass
Cold beneath the ass
Color sterling silver but is real
Unlike jewelry because its metal or steel
A cell you fix up and call your bedroom
Where it need cleaning some
I am telling you what is true
That inmate could be you
Mirrors on walls face inside like sardine cans
The blurriness can't let you see yourself as a man
Four times a day you will hear a whistle
On the mountain top not saying bullets out of a pistol
When a nigga was on the streets
Or using because of money he couldn't keep
Sergeant or C.O.. count your boys
The blow is serious full of noise still in your cell
When they point be quiet because it is hell
Better not run or try to escape
It is just as bad as a nigga inside accused of rape
It's not like going to the hole
Its up inside you—you know
You also can't eat behind
After you get your food at the mess hall line
Do your time that's your ability
In Malone, New York at Bare Hill Facility.

Footnote: Gary Lee Williams housed at Bare Hill Facility in Malone, New York fall of 2011 until Jan. 2, 2014.

Ghost Town

Since brother you have been gone so long
Many have passed away from the weakness to the strong
No one is born here to stay
We will have a day
When I go down
Where my family is it looks like ghost town
I told you before many family and friends died
To the length of my arms open wide.

A Natural Writer

I write whatever comes to mind
I take my time
Dealing with myself and talents
Hoping to be rich one day or somewhere on a island
When I started this book
I didn't have to look
On a computer or in a dictionary
I don't have to worry
I must continue this level head and look at life brighter
I wrote this from the heart, cause I am a natural writer.

My Love for the Support

A nation wide lecture
For some I never met you
And those who know me
I don't know how my future gonna be
I want to enjoy the rest of my life
But do it right
Thanks for spending money on my book out of your pockets
As for my writing I am not gonna stop it
But whatever comes to thought
I give all my love for your support.

Love for My Hate

I love my haters
The love I have for you all seems to be greater
Babies you are busybodies
Critical thoughts of me and one-sided
I always speak what is on my mind
For you, I don't have time
I only want money
Acknowledge I know how to get on it
I will not be seeing any of you later
I just love you haters.

Back Home

I can't remember how I made it
But my mother and father had separated
I went through everything became cocky
The relationship between my parents was rocky
My mother moved to Richmond, Virginia in 1987
I was a teenager not eleven
I made friends pretty fast
But the friendship didn't last
Making fake I.D.s scheming off people thoughts
And wallets
The sirens, gunshots, sounds louder than a baby with
colics
I ran the streets hard
No time for family dinners with corn on the cob
All I wanted to do was party and raise hell with rage
At such a young age
Stabbing people with knives
Blood running cuts risking their lives
No smiles, no fun times doing this
On my mind I had a list
My time was running out
Trying to eliminate bitches who thought they had clout
My troubles wasn't alone
I had company involved so I had to go back home.

Footnote: I went home from Richmond, Virginia to Fredericksburg, Virginia

Closure of Twenty Years

I am about to end this reading
That kept your brain feeding
From words put together making rhymes
On notebook paper blue lines
I want to thank God for allowing my fingers to write
Open my eyes to create this in sight
I appreciate all of you for listening
To poems I wrote non-fiction
Don't forget keep your hearts near
About the book called 20 years.

CPSIA information can be obtained
at www.ICGtesting.com
Printed in the USA
LVHW080809130323
741431LV00010B/364